Soul Ties
More Than You Imagine

Marsha Benton

DMJ Publishing & Web Design

First Edition Copyright © 2017 by Marsha Benton

ISBN 10: 0-9980959-2-3
ISBN 13: 978-0-9980959-2-9

All rights reserved. This book or any portion thereof may not be reproduced or used in any manner whatsoever without the express written permission of the publisher except for the use of brief quotations in a book review.

Published by:
DMJ Publishing & Web Design
www.dmjpublishing.com

Available from Amazon.com and other retail outlets

Cover design by:
Donna M. Jacobs
dmjpub@gmail.com

Printed in the United States of America
First Printing, 2017

All scripture references are from The Holy Bible, New King James Version and New Living Translation

DEDICATION

This book is dedicated to my illustrious parents, Walter and Carrie Benton, who instilled in me the virtues of dedication, perseverance and commitment. They relentlessly encouraged me to strive for excellence throughout my life. They have actively supported me in my determination to maximize my potential and make contributions to the world that will be a blessing to others. Everything good that comes out of my life is due to your models, guidance, wisdom, and love. Thank you for all the words of encouragement and push for tenacity that cause me to achieve goals. During this journey they have supported me at my highest and most celebrated moments as well as the lowest times in my life. Never judging; Always loving!

Above all, to Our All Mighty, All Powerful, All Knowing God, I THANK Him for choosing and equipping me with ALL I need to fulfill this wonderful Purpose & Destiny.

Love you all so very, very much,

The Queen,

Marsha

Introduction

Let me start by saying "Thank You" for purchasing this material and thinking enough of yourself and your family to seek answers. Anything that is an intricate part of your transformation helps everyone you come in contact with. I have done an in-depth study on this topic of the "SOUL TIE" because very few people give us detailed information that will make us seek the healing and deliverance needed to conquer this thing. It is more serious than we have been taught and has much more power than we imagine.

Many people have no clue as to why they act and think in certain manners or feel differently in certain atmospheres, during certain times and around particular people. They think it is anger, past experiences or the way they were raised. And it could be; BUT, it could very well be a soul tie in operation. Many are in denial about the state they are in and that makes it harder to heal and move forward in life. Many are seeking, and have sought, fulfillment in relationships to no avail. Could it be that you are unfulfilled because of Soul Ties that bring on dysfunction which in turn incapacitate you – making it difficult, if not almost impossible, to maintain healthy, wholesome, meaningful relationships?

Contents

WHAT IS A SOUL TIE?..................................... 9
SOUL TIES, DRUGS AND SUPER GLUE................... 11
WHAT IS AN UNHEALTHY SOUL TIE?................... 13
EDUCATION, INFORMATION AND ILLUMINATION..... 21
CONVICTION VERSUS CONDEMNATION 25
MY PERSONAL REVELATION AND DELIVERANCE...... 27
HEALING AND DELIVERANCE 29
STRESS – THE SILENT KILLER 33
OUR PATTERN AND GOD'S PATTERN 37
ARTICULATE TO ACTIVATE............................. 43
PRAYER OF DELIVERANCE AND INSTRUCTIONS....... 47

WHAT IS A SOUL TIE?

Terri Savelle Foy in "4 Indicators of Wrong Soul Ties" states, "A soul tie is an emotional bond or connection that unites you with someone else."

Danielle Tate in "Soul Ties How to Break Them and Live in Freedom" says:

> A soul tie is defined as a Spiritual connection between two (or more) people who have been physically intimate with each other or who have had an intense emotional or spiritual association or relationship. If you think of sex inside the confines of marriage, this is a wonderful thing. God created us to have sexual relations with our spouse that, in turn, create deep-rooted bonds.

See, He knew that after the honeymoon there'd be morning breath, bills to pay, kids to raise and dirty socks left on the floor. He knew life would happen. Therefore, He created us to be deeply bonded with our spouse so that during the crazy seasons of life, when we sometimes don't really like our spouse, we would still be deeply bonded to them.

SOUL TIES, DRUGS AND SUPER GLUE

Terri Savelle Foy states:

> When we have a sexual experience, our brains produce dopamine, the same chemical that feeds a gambling addiction, your chocolate cravings and the junkie's need for another fix. Dopamine is often described as the "feel good" chemical of the brain and it plays a major role in our lives (good and bad). You see, our bodies don't care if it's cocaine, a cupcake or a sexual experience – dopamine will be produced and it will bind us. This is why my former boyfriends were like my drug of choice and why I could not see myself without them. I was addicted to the high. I had created soul ties when I had these feel good intimate experiences with guys I wasn't married to. This is also why it literally hurt when we broke up.

Soul ties are like super glue. If you've had sexual encounters outside of marriage, consensual or forced, there is most likely a lingering soul tie that needs to be dealt with. Otherwise, you'll forever be plagued with thoughts, feelings and even actions that are unwanted. I mention forced encounters because, although pleasure is not associated with abuse, our brains still produce chemical reactions and our soul can still be tied to someone who has abused us. Some symptoms of lingering soul ties include:

- Someone whose voice you hear in your head
- Obsessive daytime thoughts about someone
- Dreaming or waking up at night thinking about someone on a regular basis
- Someone you think of or "see" in your mind when you are intimate with your spouse

WHAT IS AN UNHEALTHY SOUL TIE?

Many of us have mistaken an unhealthy soul tie for Love. We keep returning to unhealthy and toxic relationships be it an ex-lover, a family member, a girlfriend, a guy friend, a co-worker, a church member, etc. We say in our minds, "I just love them" or "God has given me a love for them and wants me to help them." (That could be the case "sometimes"; pray & Listen.) Most of the time it is our own desire or an unhealthy soul tie that keeps us returning and reconnecting with these people only to find out; yet "again", it is a toxic situation. If you are not being affected "Positively", back off.

Like the words "rapture" and "trinity", the term "soul tie" is not in scripture. However, the words "knit together" (1 Sam. 18:1, Col. 2:2 & 19, I Chron. 12:17) and the phrases "members of one another" and "all the members" are (Rom 12:5, 1 Cor. 12:26). God gave us the ability to possess this amazing bond at different levels with friends, family and companions so that we would be able to bless one another. He designed companionship/marriage to be a blessing of protection from ungodly soul ties. The soul tie in and of itself is not a bad thing. It is when the soul is tied to someone who is outside of God's design for a godly soul tie that the connection is perverted. Then it becomes a gateway for other ungodly spirits to enter in and puts us on a path of destruction.

Whole-Person Counseling.Org in "Breaking Unhealthy Soul Ties" has affirmed that:

1. An unhealthy soul tie may occur with anyone abandoned by their father or mother and they have resentment or hate toward their parents. The person may also feel compelled to find and force himself or herself into an unwanted relationship.

2. An unhealthy soul tie often comes out of the sin of fornication. Fornication is a sexual relationship before marriage. The individual will often compare their sexual partner with the person they marry.

3. An unhealthy soul tie can develop in marriage where there are co-dependent or possessive relationships.

4. An unhealthy soul tie often develops when a young adult or older adult becomes solely dependent upon his or her parents.

5. An unhealthy soul tie occurs when someone has offended us and we are holding unforgiveness toward them.

6. An unhealthy soul tie occurs when someone holds on to someone who is dying or continues to hold on to the person after their death.

7. An unhealthy soul tie occurs when someone holds on and tries to control (or fix) their children after they reach adulthood.

8. An unhealthy soul tie may form when someone idolizes another individual.

9. An unhealthy soul tie often occurs through divorce and remarriage. In the new marriage, one will often have an unhealthy soul tie to their previous marriage partner either through love or hate.

10. An unhealthy soul tie may develop through an intensive dating relationship. It may become very hurtful to one or both individuals when love is not reciprocated and there is a breakup.

11. An unhealthy soul tie will develop anytime there is an adulterous relationship. There can be an emotional attachment as well as a sexual relationship.

Great Bible Study.Com states:

> **An unhealthy soul tie can be formed with musicians groups through their music if you become obsessed with the music, which explains the strong pull towards certain music that seems almost irresistible.**

I need to talk about soul ties 3, 4, and 7 a bit more before we move on since these soul ties are very often said to be something other than what they are – much due to the people involved. Mothers to sons, sons to mothers, daughters to mothers, mothers to daughters, sons to fathers, fathers to sons, fathers to daughters, daughters to fathers, grandchildren to grandparents and vice versa or any other family member who controls you or whom you control!

> THESE MEN ARE OFTEN THRUST INTO THE POSITION OF 'HUSBAND' RATHER THAN REMAINING A SON, DUE TO THE MOTHER'S PAIN.

Mothers and fathers who will not put their grown children out to help them develop into responsible men and women that someone would want to marry. They do not hold them accountable, correct their foul behavior, or make them pay ample lodging fees for living in their home. They take care of them as if they are still 15 years old (and, mentally, most of them are). These adult children spend hundreds and even thousands on clothes, shoes, cars, weaves and trips while their parents are paying their bills and/or helping them with their children. Additionally, many of these adult children treat their parents with little or no respect. And let's not forget cleaning up behind them and their granchildren. At the very least, these parents are enablers.

Give them a timeline and put them out of your home. You

will have peace and it will help them to become responsible adults. And, by all means, do NOT fall for the guilt trip!

Many of these adult children will never have healthy, meaningful relationships. There will always be a rift – especially with sons whose fathers abandoned their mothers. These men are often thrust into the position of 'husband' rather than remaining a son, due to the mother's pain. This repositioning throws his life and her life into an unhealthy and toxic arena in that he is now responsible for her happiness and fulfillment. She tends to now lean on him for everything so he gives, gives and gives to her and does more and more for her.

The mother often doesn't realize what she is doing because of her pain, rejection and fear. She, most of the time, will not be satisfied until she is in complete control of his life. She dictates where he will live and what/how he does what he does for her. She has little or no regard for his other obligations or who he will date (if anyone); because after all, she is looking out for her own best interest – NOT HIS! And when he doesn't do or give what she wants, she makes him feel guilty or he sends himself into a state of guilt because, after all, she is mom.

Her selfish disposition and control will force him to take on a selfish disposition and control when he pursues a relationship. This is because his 'needs' are not being met since he does the giving in that toxic 'husband' position she has put him in. He is frustrated, lonely and often sad not realizing he naively put his mother in the position his wife should occupy. She, occupying this space, will not allow him to do all that is necessary to develop a healthy, meaningful relationship with another woman (though she says she wants him to have one). Translation: he can have a relationship as long as it does not interfere with her agenda and plans for his life and ALL that he does for her.

The son – since he is subconsciously feeling cheated and his needs are longing to be fulfilled relationally – when he meets a woman tends to be in such desperate need of affection (because he has given that area to his mother), he will want the woman to give him sex quickly. He will want to control the relationship and, if he does not get his way, will get frustrated and feel that he is being cheated because he is in desperate need for affection. If he cannot have what he wants, when he wants it and how he wants it, he will end the relationship or encounter because he feels as though he is supposed to have his way with you for ALL that he does for her and anyone else to whom he is obligated. His needs and feeling this way are very valid but, because you are not his wife, it is not right for him to thrust you into all the responsibility of a wife – fulfilling his needs and making him happy while he does little or nothing for you because he is doing for her and/or them.

The reality is he is giving her/them the Best of him and wants to give you the rest of him. He doesn't even realize he is not giving 'himself' what he needs to be fulfilled. And because it is mom or family most of the time, they will never have a life nor will they have their hearts' desires fulfilled. When these people that they give all their lives to don't need them anymore (for example, when children grow up or pass away), they feel lost. Ask Holy Spirit to reveal any unhealthy soul ties to your parents or children because it is easy to be in denial about family soul ties.

Single fathers, do not allow your daughters to call themselves your woman, girlfriend or wife. Do not put her in that place or allow her to put herself in that place. For the same reasons, single mothers should not put their sons in the place that should be occupied by a significant other and/or a husband. This will minimize conflict and not send mixed signals when someone significant comes into your life. It will prevent the formation of an unhealthy Soul Tie. Many people have missed the relationships and marriages they so desired to have because of their children. Many children have learned the art of manipulation and have unhealthy soul ties to their parents. These children say they want you to be happy and have a relationship BUT what they really mean is: Mom/Dad, you can have a relationship as long as the person you are dating/in relationship with or marrying still allows me to control you and does not interfere with 'my' agenda for your time, money and life. Again, do not fall for the guilt trip! Especially with your adult children who won't think about you having a say in their relationships or situations. For many, this will be the hardest thing you will ever have to do; but it must be done for 'you' and for them. You deserve happiness, joy and a fulfilling relationship. Pray and ask for the best way to handle your situation and DO IT! Faith without works is dead. (James 2:14-26)

NOTE: This scenario is not limited to mothers and sons. It can be mothers and daughters, fathers and sons, fathers and daughters, brothers and sisters, sister to sister, brother to brother, and so on. And just because your situation does not have "all" the elements of the above scenario does not mean that you do not have an unhealthy soul tie. Again, ask Holy Spirit to reveal all soul ties.

The Soul Tie will keep you returning to abusive (physical and/or verbal), toxic relationships. You feel deep inside yourself that the treatment you are experiencing is not right or good for you but you allow this life-stealing damaging person and/or people to do the same things to you time and time again. Or if you live with them, you refuse to or cannot leave. And if you are in an abusive marriage, be it verbal abuse and/or physical abuse, there is probably an unhealthy soul tie and you may need to separate from your spouse for a time to allow God to work on both of you. God does not want His children to be abused. If you truly love yourself, you will not allow yourself to be abused! Holy Spirit cannot lie! Ask Him for direction for your situation and implement it. Again, Faith without works is dead. You have to do your part. The truth is often painful but it is the transforming power that heals us. It is time to free yourself. Let go and move on with your life. YOU deserve ALL of the abundance of a healthy relationship. God loves you and wants the BEST for you!

EDUCATION, INFORMATION AND ILLUMINATION

Our soul is made up of 3 elements: your MIND - the element of a person that controls reasoning, judgment and senses; your WILL - the element in a person used to express desire, carry out habitual action, and make choices, and your EMOTIONS - a conscious mental reaction experienced as a strong feeling toward someone accompanied by physiological and behavioral changes in the body. A TIE is a feeling that is shared by people that forms a connection between them and/or limits a person's freedom to do other things.

Toxic emotions make us a liability rather than an asset to any relationship. When you have a godly soul tie – as in marriage – there is Protection, Covering, Security, Love, and Fulfillment. When there is an ungodly soul tie, the "opposite" happens and demonic spirits have legal access to enter in and wreck your emotions, make you disillusioned in your mind, overtake your will and remove self-control. The most common spirits that enter in as a result of ungodly soul ties are (but not limited to) Rejection, Insecurity, Unfulfillment, Envy, Jealousy, a Suspicious spirit, a spirit of accusation and division, being controlling/overbearing, and impure or wicked thoughts that cause you to turn into someone you don't know. And if the spirit is there for a long time, you just think it's another part of you when in fact it is a spirit or soul tie that has been in operation for many years and sometimes for generations. These spirits and/or soul ties have the ability to overtake us periodically and we have no control over the way we think, act and feel. For years we have blamed it on having a bad day, anger, having a moment, menopause or PMS (though at times it may be, because these are very real). But due to the fact that we don't understand "why" this is happening and "where" it is coming from, it just may be an ungodly soul tie in operation.

> **SEXUAL SOUL TIES CAN DO SEVERE DAMAGE TO YOUR MIND, WILL AND EMOTIONS.**

Sexual soul ties can do severe damage to your mind, will and emotions. They can be hard to detect because they first manifest so many other issues that are connected to them. Consider the way you feel when you are hurt in any relationship. Do you have little or no control over your actions or what you say? Do you react with extreme behavior? Consider the behavior of the people you've been in relationship with or are in a relationship with now. If they repeatedly cheat on you or cannot commit, they are fragmented because they have given much of themselves away sexually and they will be unable to commit until they are set free, healed and delivered. They may have soul ties that need to be broken. Free yourself from these people and pray for them. Let me say this, there may be other reasons they cannot commit, parental rejection, molestation and abandonment may be issues as well.

IMPORTANT NOTE: There is "NO LIMIT" or Bottom to the sexual soul tie. It keeps going deeper and deeper. It "never" ends. Unless it is stopped, there is always another level – porn, adding another person or people to sexual encounters which lead to male on male and female on female sexual encounters, orgies, sex with animals, drugs, etc. It keeps going because something else or someone else can always be added to the mix. The devil wants you out of control with the worst things that the world has to offer. Lasciviousness (lewd and lustful desire) is a product and result of ungodly soul ties.

Many of us tell ourselves (and we've been told) that because we intend to get married and because our hearts are right toward God that everything will be alright. Not so! You could be in for a long tumultuous ride. Even if that is the truth, it is your soul (your mind, will and emotions) that is in jeopardy and your relationship could be headed for disaster.

CONVICTION VERSUS CONDEMNATION

Now, do pay attention to "Conviction" which is given by Holy Spirit and is very different from "Condemnation."

Conviction, in the believer, brings an awareness of sin and results in repentance, confession and cleansing.

But what exactly do we mean by the term conviction? Conviction means "the act or process of convincing", "the state of being convinced" or "a fixed or strong belief". Thus, by biblical conviction, we mean convictions or beliefs derived from and based on a commitment to Scripture (the Bible). As God's Holy Word, it is the absolute index for the whole of our lives – faith and practice.

Conviction refers to the state of being convinced and confident that something is true. It means a strong persuasion or belief. In other words, conviction stands opposed to doubt and skepticism. When we think of a man of conviction, we also think in terms of action and direction. We think of a person whose convictions have a definite impact on how he lives, on what he does/says and where he goes. By a man of biblical convictions, we mean a man whose convictions are derived from Scripture and whose convictions affect him scripturally.

> **Biblical conviction is really the product of three things that characterize the ideal Christian leader or the person of maturity: (a) a commitment to Scripture as one's authority, (b) the construction of specific beliefs and convictions based on that authority, and (c) the courage to act on those convictions in faith. (Biblia.com)**

"Condemnation" is declaring an evildoer to be guilty and can refer to the punishment inflicted on man because of that guilt. Without Jesus, mankind stands condemned before God not only because of the sin of Adam (Rom. 5:16-18) but also because of our own sin (Matt. 12:37). DO NOT go into condemnation when you do something you know is not right. Immediately ask God for forgiveness and why you did it (if you don't know). Only God knows the exact day and time of your deliverance. Thank Him in advance for it as well as for His wonderful Grace and Mercy that covers you and keep moving forward in life fulfilling your purpose, destiny and being a Blessing to the Kingdom! "There is therefore now no condemnation for those who are in Christ Jesus. For the law of the Spirit of life in Christ Jesus has set you free from the law of sin and of death," (Rom. 8:1-2). Christians have passed out of condemnation because they are forgiven in Christ.

MY PERSONAL REVELATION AND DELIVERANCE

My first deliverance came around the time Dr. Juanita Bynum preached "No More Sheets". During that time my fiancé and I would have sex then I would get up right after we were done, go take a bath and go into my living room to get on my knees and pray! Imagine what that did to him!? During the time I was praying about my actions toward my fiancé, I would be very emotional, overbearing, judgmental and controlling. I had asked God why I was seemingly out of control emotionally. I didn't know about soul ties at that time. I had heard the term but that was all. I had no idea he was having sex with a woman in another state. The Lord let me know! He's good like that! Shortly afterwards, the Lord told me to break it off. I told the Lord I couldn't because I loved him too much so the Lord had him break up with me. That is when my soul tie fully manifested. I thought about him all the time. I lost weight.

I couldn't sleep. I would drive by his house and his job. I would sit where I knew he'd be. Then the devil reminded me that I had the spare key to his car. Yup, I took his car! Just sitting in it gave me a high and a feeling of satisfaction – for a moment and only for a moment – because when that encounter was over, I wanted another. I hid his car around the corner from where he lived. That, in turn, made him call me which was what I wanted because he had cut off all communication with me and the Lord wouldn't allow me to call him. I wasn't thinking right; the soul tie had overtaken me. My mind, will and emotions were a wreck. I had stolen a police officer's car! Yes! My fiancé was a police officer. Thank God he didn't turn me in. He called me for the car. It was during this relationship that I knew something was wrong because I kept saying to myself "that ain't me; I don't do those kinds of things!" That spirit/soul tie would make me feel guilty and ashamed of my actions. That's what those spirits do. They attack you while using you to attack and destroy others. Watch the movie "Fallen" with Denzel Washington to get a picture of how the subtle transference of spirits can change you and greatly impact your life.

Soon after, the Lord told me to study "Soul Ties" and said I was going to help myself and others get freed from this pit.

Consider the things you've done and the behavior you've been displaying. Ask Holy Spirit to reveal any and all soul ties.

HEALING AND DELIVERANCE

Get serious about your deliverance; your family's deliverance could begin with you. The generational curse is broken off of your family but the curse's influence may still be lingering. First and foremost, FORGIVE! FORGIVE and let go of the person or people who have hurt you in any relationship. Ask Holy Spirit to reveal the people you need to forgive.

Soul ties may have to be broken in phases and stages so don't get discouraged if you don't see immediate results. It may take a while but it will happen. The key is to keep seeking God about the soul ties. Great Bible Study.Com suggests that if gifts were given to you by the other person in connection with the sin or unholy relationship – such as rings, flowers, cards, bras, etc. – get rid of them. Such things symbolize the ungodly relationship and can hold a soul tie in place. Note: This does not need to be done in every situation. Ask Holy Spirit to reveal to you what (if anything) you need to get rid of.

We often use the Scripture in 1 Corinthians 6: 18a, "Run from sexual sin! Or Flee fornication!" This scripture has been thrown at many of us for years with no other instructions other than "run from the situation" and "don't do it!" It was always spoken in a way that made us feel even guiltier and condemned – driving us deeper into emotional turmoil and making us feel unworthy of the blessings of God. Many of us would flee one fornicating situation only to run right into another one...relationship after relationship, year after year. The saying, "looking for love in all the wrong places", is certainly true when there are ungodly soul ties in operation. None of us wanted to displease God. We really did want to be and do right in His sight; we were just not well-informed on "how to" flee fornication and be victorious in this area. The grace of God was not mentioned to be the covering and sustainer we needed to walk through the situation and flee fornication effectively!

The correct way to flee fornication is through the "Love of Jesus Christ and God's Love for us." Study it, meditate on it, speak it, and renew your mind with it. Be transformed by the renewing of your mind (Romans 12:2). Every decision we make and every goal that is attained is first settled in our mind. ALL changes, good or bad, began with a thought.....

Revelation of your situation will come as you seek God for your healing and deliverance. Ask God for a safe place or person to help you through your process if you feel the need or if Holy Spirit prompts you to seek help. For many of us, soul ties were formed as a result of being raped and/or molested and many other elements manifest. Get help!

We were 'created' for intimacy and relationship. Most of the time, the act of fornication overshadows our need and desire for intimacy. I cannot recall anyone ever saying to me or connecting my need or desire for intimacy with my sexual relationships. One was always separated from the other unless the subject of marriage was the topic.

STRESS – THE SILENT KILLER

Stress is a negative thought. Negative self-talk, strong emotions, anxiety, fear, anger, and resentment lead the charge and the body subconsciously follows thus physical manifestations begin to surface. It is important to recognize stress-related issues (i.e. skin outbreaks, hair loss, weight gain, weight loss, stomach, bowel and female issues to name a few). We can stress ourselves when healing and deliverance do not come when we think they should. Give yourself time to 'process' the new information and additional time to 'embrace' the changes we are looking to make. When insufficient time is given to mentally process change and anything outside the norm, you can get discouraged. Know that God's grace will sustain you through the process. Channeling emotions through positive thought helps to manage stress and feelings of depression while minimizing condemnation.

I am adamant about being mindful of your thought process

because, as Joyce Meyer says, "Where the Mind goes the Man will follow!" Don't think about where you are, think about where you want to go!

We can stress ourselves when an encounter or association doesn't turn into the relationship we so desire to have. Identify the activities that help you to decompress or relax when you are stressed (that are not sexual in nature). For me, it is outdoor activities. I also love to dance. And I love walking alone or with friends – walking maximizes the benefits of having a healthy body and it clears the mind. Prayer walking aligns your mind, body, soul and spirit. Proverbs 16:24 says, "Gracious words are a honeycomb, sweet to the soul and healing to the bones." Meditating on the Word of God or positive things stimulates creativity. Our positive words and affirmations eradicate negative, stressful and destructive thinking. In addition, it promotes a peaceful atmospheric change which causes dopamine to be released that puts one in a happy, healthy, healing state of mind.

> **OUR POSITIVE WORDS AND AFFIRMATIONS ERADICATE NEGATIVE, STRESSFUL AND DESTRUCTIVE THINKING.**

Other stress relieving activities include things as simple as closing your eyes and taking deep breaths. My all-time favorite stress reliever is LAUGHING! Joy promotes laughter and laughter is like medicine. Laughter relieves stress, boosts immunity, improves your mood and puts you in a happy place. So, by all means, Laugh! Laugh! And Laugh some more! The Bible says, "A CHEERFUL HEART IS GOOD MEDICINE BUT A CRUSHED SPIRIT DRIES UP THE BONES" (Proverbs 17:22). God wants us to be happy and joyful in our present state, whatever it may be. "THE JOY OF THE LORD IS OUR STRENGTH" (Nehemiah 8:10c).

OUR PATTERN AND GOD'S PATTERN

OUR PATTERN

On a personal note, I could not wear thong underwear for a few years because they were a signal to my body that I was going to have sex. At that time, I only wore them when I was going out with my man and I knew the night would end in a hot sexual encounter. After we broke up, when I would wear my thongs, I would get emotional and by the end of the night I would be sad. I asked the Lord why this was happening and my answer came the next time I wore them. I felt my body shift! I immediately took them off and I felt my body shift again back to normal. Holy Spirit reminded me of the connection and I understood at once! I did not get rid of them; I just put them in the back of the drawer until I was free from the soul tie. All is well now!

When we recognize and identify soul ties during our process, we are able to understand 'when' and 'why' emotions and feelings arise at certain times, in certain settings or around certain people. If you still have feelings of anger or sadness around certain people, you could have a soul tie and/or unforgiveness. Your emotions feed on EVERY touch, call, text and word that comes from the people with whom you have soul ties.

Moreover, we may break the soul tie and walk in the freedom of God for a period of time or until we enter another intimate relationship. Upon being sexually intimate in the new relationship, another soul tie may be formed. If this occurs, start your healing and deliverance process all over again. I would do it even if there were no signs of a soul tie to cover myself and alleviate my soul from the seed of a soul tie as soon as possible.

> **DO NOT GO INTO CONDEMNATION AND BEAT YOURSELF UP, NOR SHOULD YOU ALLOW THE ENEMY TO BEAT YOU DOWN.**

DO NOT go into condemnation and beat yourself up, nor should you allow the enemy to beat you down. I will keep saying this because that was my battle for many years and it caused me to stop some good things from flowing in my life because Faith can't flow through condemnation. This revelation answered many questions I had about why things were held up and not manifesting in my life. (Thank you Apostle Troy Grant for this information.)

Do not allow your mind to stay in a condemning state. God LOVES YOU and ONLY HE knows how long it will take to deliver you. Just stay in His face no matter what you are doing or how you are feeling and seek His wisdom for your situation. He is STILL going to bless you!

Learn to receive the "GRACE" of God for all areas in which you are challenged! The GRACE OF GOD sustains us through our healing and deliverance processes but we must 'TAKE HOLD OF IT'. That means meditating, believing and speaking what God says about you over and over again. Post inspirational phrases in places you frequent while refusing to allow condemnation to overtake you. This is what I have done for years and it works! The GRACE liberates us and enables us to move forward to fulfill our purpose and destiny without guilt and shame. If we do not take the GRACE, we remain in an unhealthy state and become paralyzed which brings on stagnation. We can remain in bondage for many, many years because FAITH cannot flow through condemnation. Father God, by Faith we receive YOUR GRACE today; and we receive every blessing and good gift You have for us by Faith, in Jesus name! (Thank you Pastor Sadie Brunson for this information)

By now I know many of you are saying, "Why didn't she just say stay away from relationships if they cause you to fornicate?" Abstinence is not healing and deliverance. You can stay away from relationships and sex for many years.

But the first time you enter into another relationship, you will end up in a sexual encounter; because, again, abstinence cannot heal or deliver you.

Making a commitment to abstain is good for some people. But for others, it gives them a false sense of their reality and could cause them to be in a cycle of condemnation, regret, feelings of being a failure, depression and oppression each time they enter into a sexual relationship outside of marriage. That is what happened to me. The reality/truth is, many of us abstain until the opportunity 'we desire' comes along again. Just because your standards are higher than others or you are 'particular' about who you enter into relationship with does not, by any means, affirm that you are NOT a soul tie victim.

Analyze each relationship you are or were in. Now that you have some information, look for the signs of a soul tie (also see the Whole Person Counseling list of 11 soul ties). Pray the prayer I have provided at the end of the book over those soul ties.

Unrealistic expectations can send one spiraling and cause additional emotional turmoil or stress which comes from our thought patterns. Be more mindful of the way you think during the process. Do not allow your mind to focus on the negative aspects of your life! Think positive and be optimistic. Whatsoever things are of good report, think on these things (Phil. 4:8). God wants us to do great things; however, great things are not done by chance or on impulse but by a series of 'little' changes brought together to achieve goals.

GOD'S PATTERN

The foundation of your relationships needs to be built on God's love and will for your life. More often than not, we only truly seek God when we have exhausted all other means. Wisdom seeks God "first" to minimize failure or disaster. We either plan to succeed or we plan to fail. There is no in-between. Write the vision and make it plain (Hab. 2:2). What do you desire in relationships? Write it. Speak it. Pray it.

God's revelation of your situation will help you understand His patterns and move forward. Personal development of any kind, with rewards and purpose, provides a paradigm for reaching goals and helps us stay positively focused. As you learn more about yourself during times of transition and transformation, it should be connected to rewards and promotion. Know that because you have read this book you are better informed and postured for victory and armed with the information needed to be victorious in this area. So rejoice and reward yourself! Celebrate yourself. Compliment yourself. And, by all means, learn to love yourself. Many of us say we love ourselves; however, people who love themselves do not allow themselves to be abused.

ARTICULATE TO ACTIVATE

Great Bible Study.com suggests: "Any rash vows or commitments made that played a part in forming the soul tie should be renounced and repented of, and broken in Jesus' name."

Even things like "I will love you forever" or "I could never love another man (or woman)!" need to be renounced. They are spoken commitments that need to be undone verbally. As Proverbs 21:23 tells us, "Whoso keepeth his mouth and his tongue keepeth his soul from troubles." The tongue has the ability to bring the soul great troubles and bondage. Even sayings like, "I love you with all of my heart." The only One you should be loving with 'all' your heart is God.

Speak the Word of God out of your mouth out loud daily. It will hasten the process. PRAY EFFECTIVE PRAYERS and believe God for the results. I will not give specific numbers of times to do this. It's personal. You will have good days and bad days. The soul ties will have you on an emotional roller coaster. On the bad days and weeks, you will need to speak over yourself more during those times than others. But by all means, keep pressing toward the mark and believe that the goal is attainable. Again, you may not notice any change but know that change is happening. Healing and deliverance is happening. Believe that it is! Listen to Holy Spirit. He will lead and guide you into all TRUTH (John 16:13). Trust Him – even when you don't understand where He's leading you. You are fearfully and wonderfully made (Psalm 139:14). Your process may not be like anyone else's. You are unique and there is only one "you!" God created you; therefore, only He knows the plan for you. Seek Him for direction every day and allow God's love to permeate your mind and emotions.

> **FOR SOME, THE PROCESS IS LONGER THAN OTHERS DEPENDING ON YOUR LIFE EXPERIENCES.**

God will allow situations to cross your path to let you know where you are in the process, what you need to work on and speak over as well as the progress you've made.

John 14:16-17 states, "And I will ask the Father, and he will give you another Advocate, who will never leave you. He is the Holy Spirit, who leads into all truth."

For some, the process is longer than others depending on

your life experiences. For some, the healing process could be slow and painful, especially if the relationship does not end the way we desired it to end. And, if we become disappointed in God and go into denial about our true feelings, we cover up with religious actions and attitudes which add to the length of the healing and deliverance process. Are you covering disappointment in God? I was. Are you covering your pain and soul tie with religious actions? I was.

Ask Holy Spirit to reveal it to you. Ask right now. For some, the healing process will be instantaneous. We are all different and God knows each of us by name. He also knew how long your healing and deliverance process would be thousands of years before you were born. So 'do not' allow condemnation to arise. And when disappointment creeps in, cast it down with the Word of God:

I have the mind of Christ (1 Cor. 2:16)

I can do all things through Christ Who strengthens me (Phil. 4:13)

With God, all things are possible (Matt. 19:26)

I am the righteousness of God through Christ Jesus our Lord (2 Cor. 5:21)

I am more than a Conqueror (Rom. 8:37)

But you are a chosen generation, a royal priesthood, a holy nation, His own special people, that you may proclaim the praises of Him who called you out of darkness into His marvelous light; who once were not a people but are now the people of God, who had not obtained mercy but now have obtained mercy. (1 Peter 2:9-10)

Entrepreneurs 10 Characteristics of Superior Leaders states:

> **The people with a mission, vision, goal, strong support system, a 'can-do' attitude coupled with inspiration and ambition are some of the characteristics of superior leaders. With each endeavor, large or small, spiritual or natural, allow these essential traits to be your forerunners.**

Again, know that God is working on your behalf. He is not disappointed in you. He is not out to beat you down for every mistake you make. He knew the end from the beginning. He knew how long it would take for you to be healed, set free and delivered. The ONLY thing that is stopping you from receiving your healing is "you" not making up your mind to do so. What are 'you' going to do? BELIEVE that the best is still yet to come for you and your latter days will be greater than your former days. The healing and deliverance process has already begun! God can't wait to Bless your socks off and He will give you the desires of your heart! Apostle Wynell Freeman said, "When you get rid of the trash, God will give you the treasure!"

PRAYER OF DELIVERANCE AND INSTRUCTIONS

THE PRAYER

Lord Jesus, I am asking You to come into my heart and be Lord over every area of my life. Teach me Your ways and to hear Your voice. Father, I renounce any and all ungodly soul ties formed between myself and anyone as a result of connections, relationships, rape, molestation, fornication, sex with _____ (name people) and other sexual encounters I have had throughout my life. Sever all inappropriate and diabolical soul ties and entanglements. I employ the Angelic hosts to fight for and protect me. Every stronghold is broken off of my mind. My will and my emotions are now stabilized and at peace. I have the mind of Christ. Condemnation has no place in my life and must go now! I am blessed and highly favored of God. The flow of Holy Spirit is perfect and unhindered in my life. I receive wisdom and instruction clearly. I command all satanic influences to be shattered and I break them now.

I speak that seeds of righteousness, love, peace, wisdom, wealth and joy replace all demonic strongholds. I give the enemy no access to me and nothing will interfere with my healing, deliverance and advancement. And now unto Him Who is able to exceed abundantly above all I could ask or think, according to the power at work in me, in the mighty name of Jesus. It is so!

INSTRUCTIONS:

1. Purchase John Eckhart's book: Prayers that Rout demons. Pray those prayers that pertain to the Soul Tie and all the other spirits I listed.

2. Purchase Cindy Trimm's book & CD: Rules of Engagement. These are Warfare Prayers. I also recommend Dr. Cindy Trimm's "Atomic Power of Prayer and Prophetic Intercession". You can play the CD in your car or office and in your home. You don't have to play it loud.

3. If you have been molested, purchase "Mercy Rewrote My Life" by Sadie Brunson.

4. Do small fasts (3 days) and ask God to destroy the ungodly Soul Ties.

5. Confess the Word of God over your life daily.

About The Author

Marsha Benton is a licensed minister with a Bachelor's Degree in Organizational Dynamics. She graduated from Immaculata University, Magna Cum Laude and a member of the National Honor society Phi Beta Sigma. She is also a licensed cosmetologist in the states of Pennsylvania and Delaware. Marsha has always been creative, blessed to write, multi-gifted and multi-talented.

Marsha has been blessed to serve and lead on many levels. She has made a career in the Insurance Industry for a number of years in various capacities: Accounting, Auto Operations, and Claims. As a Change Ambassador for the region, she has worked on many special projects and taskforces to assure profitability, build awareness and create buy-in to enhancements with a track record of excellence during her tenure. Since 1998, she has been a coordinator for several conferences with 100 to 10,000 individuals in attendance and up to 200 volunteers. Marsha has also coordinated several weddings and social affairs throughout her lifetime. As a Kingdom Consultant, she has assisted several churches in a number of leadership roles and responsibilities including church start-up, administration and conference consulting. In the last few years she has been working on her brand which will be formally introduced in the coming year. God has positioned her to be a Campaign Consultant in the political arena which she views as an opportunity to insert God in areas in which He wants to make a difference.

Marsha enjoys helping people, traveling, outdoor activities, bowling, roller skating and spending time with friends and family.

Contact Information: MBENTON2016@OUTLOOK.COM, www.facebook.com/marsha.benton.35

More Than You Imagine

Please let me know how this book has impacted your life by leaving a review on www.amazon.com. I would love to hear from you.

www.ingramcontent.com/pod-product-compliance
Lightning Source LLC
Chambersburg PA
CBHW061516040426
42450CB00008B/1642